Batch Script Programming

Narendra Dwivedi

DEDICATION

I Would Like To Dedicate This Book To My Parents

Thank You For Purchasing The Book

Start Learning Batch Script With This Complete Practical Book

TABLE OF CONTENT

About This Book

CMD Is A Very Useful Tool Available In Windows Operating System Using Which We Can Perform Many Actions. By Using Batch Script Programming, We Can Execute Commands In Command Line Interpreter ,i.e. Command Prompt. In This Book We Will Learn About Batch Script Programming From Beginner To Advance Level.

Batch Script

Batch Script Is A Simple Plain Text File Which Contain Series Of Commands Which Will Be Further Executed In Sequence By Command Line Interpreter.

Generally Batch Script Is Also Known As **Batch File**. Batch Files Are Not Commonly Used As Programming Language But Very Few Of Us Are Aware Of Its Dominance In Windows Operating System. We Can Do Almost Everything When We Know Relevant Command Line Instruction.

Lets See What Are The Requirements In Order To Create A Batch File. To Create A Batch File Firstly We Require A Windows Operating System Because Batch File Can Be Executed Only In Windows Operating System. After That, To Write Codes Or Command , We Need A Text Editor. For This Purpose You Can Use Notepad++(recommended) / Sublime Text / Visual Studio Code.
Lets Talk About Some Advantages Of Batch File :

- Uses Less Memory As Compared To Other Interface Because It Has Command Line Interface.
- It Needed Fewer Resources
- It Can Run On Lower Resolution Screen
- It Is Faster & Can Handle Tasks Easily.

Hello World In Batch Script

Batch File Opens Command Prompt To Execute The Code In The Sequence. Do You Know Where Command Prompt Exists ? It Exist In C:\Windows\System32 Folder With Name cmd.exe . Additionally, You Can Also Open It From Run (Windows Key +R) By Entering cmd Then Pressing Enter Button. By Default , CMD Has Black Background & White Foreground.

```
C:\Windows\System32\cmd.exe
Microsoft Windows [Version 10.0.19043.928]
(c) Microsoft Corporation. All rights reserved.

C:\Windows\System32>
```

For Printing Text On Screen, **echo** Command Followed By Text To Be Printed Is Used.

Example :

echo Hello World

Output :

```
C:\Users\ND>echo Hello World
Hello World
```

Lets Create Our First Batch File. For That Open Any Text Editor (I Am Using Notepad++) And Enter Following Code

Code :

echo Hello World
pause

Explanation :

In The Above Code I Have Used **echo** Command To Print Or Display Text On Screen. So It Will Print **Hello World** On Screen As After **echo** Command , I Have Written Hello World. After That I Have Used **pause** Command Which Is Used To Hold The Screen Until User Presses Any Key. If You Will Not Use **pause** Command , Then Batch File Will Be Closed Instantly On Opening.
After Writing The Code , Save The File With Any Name But Make Sure To Write **.bat** Or **.cmd** As Extension As The Extension Of Batch File Is **.bat** / **.cmd**

Output :

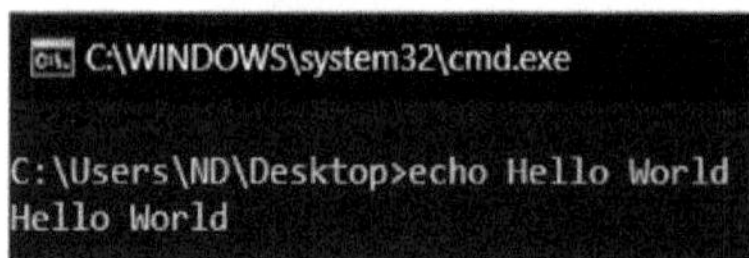

Displaying Only Output

In The Previous Output , We Can See Some Prompt & Command Along With Output Which Is Making Our Batch File Looks Bad. In Any Programming , We Always Show Only Results Or Output On The Screen. So How To Hide These Prompts & Commands From The Batch File ? For This We Have To Write **@echo off** Command On The First Line Of Our Program. This Command Will Hide All The Prompts Or Commands And Will Display Only Output.
Code :

```
@echo off
echo Hello World
pause
```

Output:

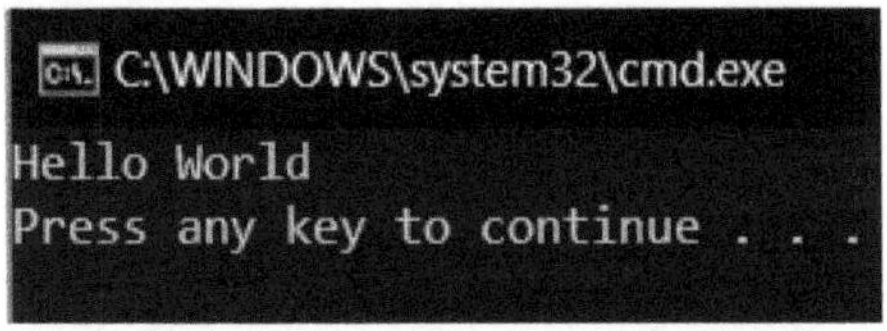

```
C:\WINDOWS\system32\cmd.exe
Hello World
Press any key to continue . . .
```

Changing Title

In The Previous Output , We Can See Location Of Command Prompt (C:\WINDOWS\system32\cmd.exe) In The Title Section. If We Want To Change The Title Then We Have To Use **title** Command Followed By Title Text. This Will Change The Title

Code :

```
@echo off
title My Program
echo Hello World
pause
```

Output :

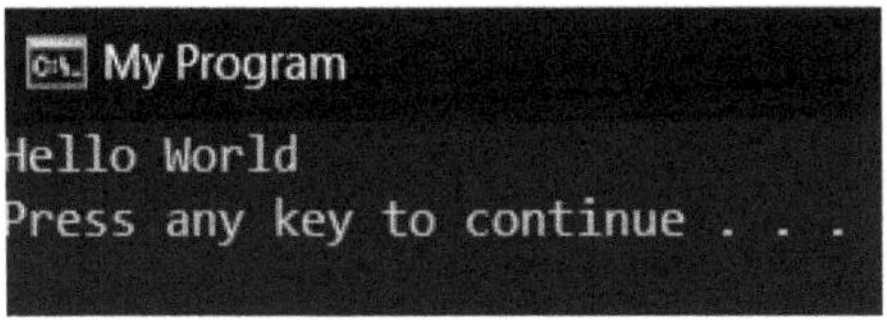

```
My Program
Hello World
Press any key to continue . . .
```

Color In Batch Script

As We Know That The Default Color Is Black For Background & White For Foreground. If You Want To Change These Default Color , Then Have To Use **color xy** Command , Where x & y Are The Value Of Color Given Below (x Is The Background Color & y Is The Foreground Color).

0 = Black	8 = Gray
1 = Blue	9 = Light Blue
2 = Green	A = Light Green
3 = Aqua	B = Light Aqua
4 = Red	C = Light Red
5 = Purple	D = Light Purple
6 = Yellow	E = Light Yellow
7 = White	F = Bright White

For Example , By Using Command **color EC** , The Background Color Will Changed To Light Yellow & Foreground Color Will Changed To Light Red.

Note : ***Most Of The Command In Batch Script Are Not Case Sensitive***

Code :

```
@echo off
title My Program
color EC
echo Hello World
pause
```

Variable

As We Know That Variables Are Important Assets Which Stores Values. To Store A Variable We Use **set** Command

Command:

set variablename=value

Where variablename Is The Name Of The Variable & value Is The Value To Be Stored In That Variable.

Example:

set myvar=Hello

To Display Value Of A Variable , We Have To Enclose The Variable With % Sign.

Example:

echo %variablename%

Code:

```
@echo off
title My Program
set myvar=Hello
echo The Value Of Variable Is %myvar%
pause
```

For Storing Numeric Value In Variable Or Performing Mathematical Operation Using Variable , We Have To Use Command **set /a variablename=value**

Example :

set /a myvar=5

Predefined & Environment Variable

There Are Some Predefined Environment Variable Which Are Widely Used. Some Of Them Are :

APPDATA	Tells Path Of Application Data
CommonProgramFiles	Tells Path Of Common Program Files
COMPUTERNAME	Tells The Name Of Computer
ProgramFiles	Tells Path Of Program Files
ProgramData	Tells Path Of Program Data
RANDOM	Generates Random Numbers Between 0 To 32,767
SYSTEMROOT	Tells Path Of System Root
TEMP or TMP	Tells Path Of Temporary Folder

USERNAME	Tells Username Of Computer
USERPROFILE	Tells The Path Of User Profile Folder
WINDIR	Tells The Path Of Windows Directory

Example :

echo Your Windows Directory Is Located At %WINDIR%

Code :

```
@echo off
title Learning Predefined Variable
echo Your Program Files Is Located At %ProgramFiles%
pause
```

Output :

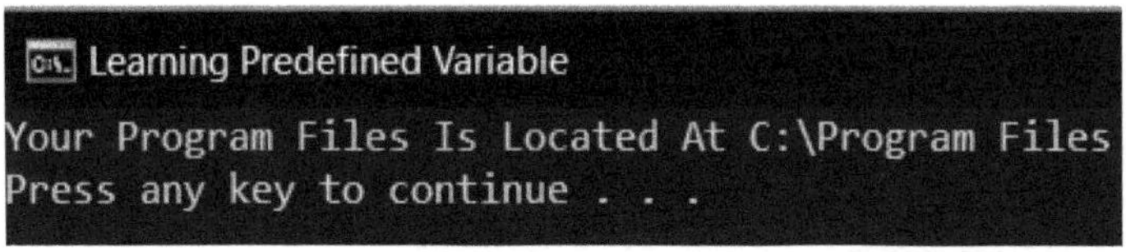

```
Learning Predefined Variable
Your Program Files Is Located At C:\Program Files
Press any key to continue . . .
```

Taking Input From User

To Take Input From User , We Need To Use command
set /p variablename=

Or

set /p variablename=Some String

Example:

set /p thename=Enter Name :

Code:

```
@echo off
title Taking Input From User
echo Enter Your Name
set /p thename=Name :
echo Welcome %thename%
pause
```

Explanation:
We Have Taken Name From The User & Stored In **thename** Variable. After That We Have Printed Value Of Variable **thename** Using %thename%

Output:

```
Taking Input From User
Enter Your Name
Name : Narendra Dwivedi
Welcome Narendra Dwivedi
Press any key to continue . . .
```

Arithmetic Operator

Arithmetic Operator Takes Operands & Perform Mathematical Operation Of Them Like Addition, Subtraction, Multiplication etc.

Operators :

+	Addition Operator
-	Subtraction Operator
*	Multiplication Operator
/	Division Operator
%	Modulus Operator

Code :

```
@echo off
title Calculator
echo Enter First Number
set /p fn=First Number :
echo Enter Second Number
set /p sn=Second Number :
set /a add=%fn%+%sn%
set /a sub=%fn%-%sn%
set /a ml=%fn%*%sn%
set /a div=%fn%/%sn%
set /a modulus=fn%%sn
echo The Result After Addition Is %add%
```

```
echo The Result After Substraction Is %sub%
echo The Result After Multiplication Is %ml%
echo The Result After Division is %div%
echo The Result After Using Modulus Operator Is %modulus%
pause
```

Explanation :

In This Above Code , We Have Taken Two Numbers From Users & Stored Them In Variable Named **fn** and **sn**. Then We Have Used Arithmetic Operator Using Command **set /a variablename=Arithmetic Operation** (For Example : set /a add=%fn%+%sn% , Here We Have Performed Addition Of Two Numbers Using **+** Operator).

Note : ***For Modulus Operator , We Need To Write FirstVariable%%SecondVariable***

Output :

```
Calculator
Enter First Number
First Number : 12
Enter Second Number
Second Number : 10
The Result After Addition Is 22
The Result After Substraction Is 2
The Result After Multiplication Is 120
The Result After Division is 1
The Result After Using Modulus Operator Is 2
Press any key to continue . . .
```

Comment

Comments Are Like Text Notes Added In The Program By The Programmer And These Comments Are Ignored By The Program

Command :

Rem Any Comment Text Here

OR

:: Any Comment Text Here

Note : ***We Can Insert Comment Using Rem Command Or Two Colons* (::)**

If Else

If Else Are Decision Making Statement Widely Used In Majority Of Programming Languages.

Command :

if condition PerformAction

or

if condition (PerformAction)

Example :

if %myvar%==hello echo Yes

Code :

```
@echo off
title If Statement
set myvar=Hello
if %myvar%==Hello echo Yes
pause
```

Output :

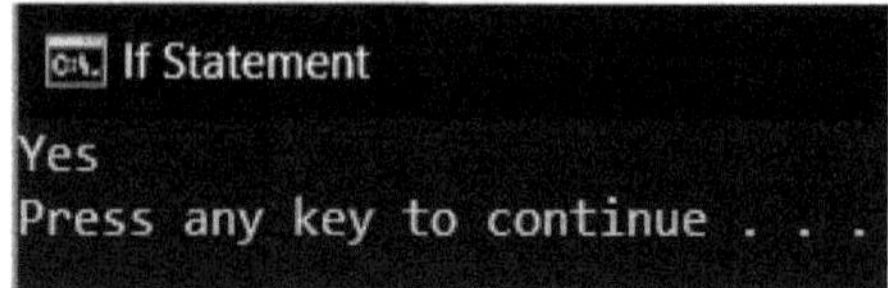

Command :

If condition (PerformAction) else (PerformAnotherAction)

Example :

if %myvar%==hello (echo Yes) else (echo No)

Code :

```
@echo off
title If Else Statement
set myvar=Hello
if %myvar%==Welcome (echo Yes) else (echo No)
pause
```

Output :

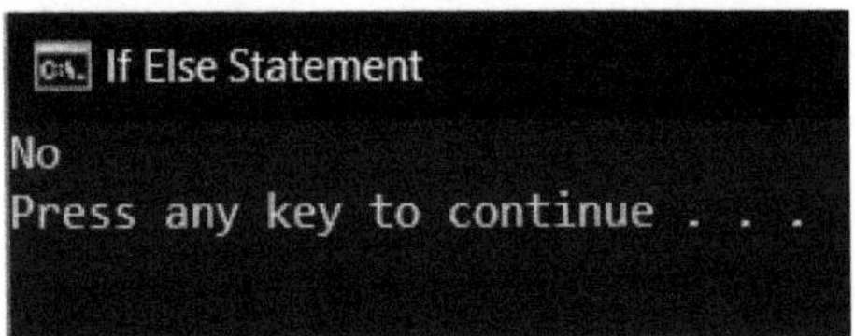

Labels & GoTo

Labels

Labels Are Like New Block In Batch Script . In Batch Scripts We Can Also Create More Than One Labels.

Command :

:labelname

Code Example :

```
@echo off
title Labels
echo Hello
pause
:flabel
echo Welcome
:slabel
echo Welcome Again
pause
```

GoTo

GoTo Is Used To Send The Program To Specified Label

Command:

```
goto labelname
```

Code Example :

```
@echo off
title Check User
:main
echo Enter Your Name
set /p thename=Name :
if %thename%==Narendra (goto showwelcome) else
(goto showerror)
:showwelcome
echo Welcome
pause
goto main
:showerror
echo Not Authorized
pause
goto main
```

Explanation :

In The Above Example , If User Will Enter 'Narendra' As Name Then Program Will Go To **showwelcome** Label Where Welcome Text Is Shown. Otherwise Program Will Go To **showerror** Label Where Not Authorized Text Will Be Shown.

Cleaning The Screen

Suppose We Want To Remove Any Previous Texts From The Screen On Going To Any Label. For This Purpose **cls** Command Is Used To Clear The Screen.

Code Example :

```
@echo off
title Check User
:main
cls
echo Enter Your Name
set /p thename=Name :
if %thename%==Narendra (goto showwelcome) else
(goto showerror)
:showwelcome
echo Welcome
pause
goto main
:showerror
echo Not Authorized
pause
goto main
```

Explanation :

In The Above Example , Whenever The Program Will Go To **main** Label , All The Previous Texts Will Be Removed Due To The Use Of **cls** Command.

Checking File Exist Or Not

To Check Whether A File Exists Or Not , We Have To Use **exist** Command

Example :

if exist “filename.extension” echo Yes It Exist

if exist “filename.extension” echo (Yes It Exist) else (echo Not Exist)

Where filename Is The Name Of The File & .extension Is The Extension Of That File. (Like **Detail.txt** , **Movie.mp4**)

Changing Directory

To Change Current Active Directory , We Need To Use **cd** Command

Command :

cd DirectoryName

Example :

cd MyNewFolder

Not Operator

Not Operator Is Used To Convert The Value From True To False.

Example :

if Not %thename%==Narendra echo Unauthorized

Explanation :

If The Value Of Variable **thename** Is Other Than Narendra , Then It Will Print **Unauthorized**

Loop

Loop Is Very Important Part Of Any Programming Language. It Helps To Reduce Many Lines Of Codes Which Makes Our Program Less Complex.

In Batch Scripts , There Is Direct Implementation Of Loop Using For Loop Only.

Command :

for %%variablename in list do something

Note :

- **Write variablename In One Character like y**
- **In Batch Scripts Loop , Variable Is Written as %%variablename Instead Of %variablename%**
- **List Is The Value For Which Loop Will Execute**

Code Example :

```
@echo off
title Loop
for %%y in (1,5,7) do echo %%y
pause
```

Output :

```
Loop
1
5
7
Press any key to continue . . .
```

Looping Through Range :

Command :

for /l %%variablename in (LowerLimit,Incremen,UpperLimit) do something

Where :

/l Specify That For Loop Is Iterating Through A Range Of Values

Code Example :

```
@echo off
title Loop
for /l %%y in (0,5,50) do echo %%y
pause
```

Output :

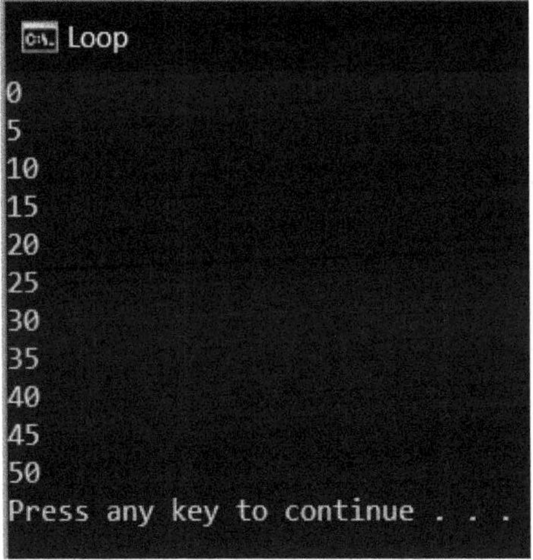

Date & Time

To Display Current Date , We Have To Use **%date%.**

For Displaying Current Time , We Have To Use **%time%**

Code Example :

```
@echo off
title Date Time
echo Current Date Is %date%
echo Current Time Is %time%
pause
```

Ping Command

It Is A Network Related Command Used To Test The Reachability Of A Host. Using This Command , We Can Also Test & Verify That If A Particular IP Address Or Web Address Exists Or Not.

Command :

ping Address

Example :

ping narendradwivedi.org

Creating Folder

To Create A Folder Using Batch Script , We Have To Use **md** Or **mkdir** Command.

Command :

md FolderName

Or

mkdir FolderName

Example :

md MyFolder

Deleting Folder

To Delete A Folder Using Batch Script , We Have To Use **rd** Or **rmdir** Command

Command :

rd FolderName

Or

rmdir FolderName

Example :

rd MyFolder

Deleting File

To Delete A File Using Batch Script , We Have To Use **del** Command

Command :

del FileName

Example :

del myfile.txt

Renaming Folder

To Rename A Folder Using Batch Script , We Have To Use **rename** Command

Command :

rename originalfoldername newfoldername

Example :

rename MyFolder MyNewFolder

Renaming File

To Rename A File Using Batch Script , We Have To Use **ren** Command

Command :

ren orignalfilenameWithExtension newfilenameWithExtension

Example :

ren myfile.txt mynewfile.txt

Overwriting & Appending In File

Lets See How To Create A File Using Batch Script & Then Write Something Into It Like Some Text.

For Overwriting Command :

echo sometext >filename.extension

Where filename Is The Name Of The File & .extension Is The Extension (Like **detail.txt**)

Greater Than Symbol (>) Will Overwrite The File (Will Remove Any Previous Content & Then Write Into It)

Code Example :

```
@echo off
title WritingIntoFiles
echo Enter Your Name
set /p thename=Name :
echo Welcome %thename% >detail.txt
pause
```

Explanation :

Above Code Will Save Text 'Welcome thename' In **detail.txt** File (Where thename Is The Value Of Variable thename) (> Will Overwrite The File That Means It Will Remove Any Previous Content)

For Appending Command :

echo sometext >>filename.extension

Where filename Is The Name Of The File & .extension Is The Extension (Like **detail.txt**)

Two Greater Than Symbol (**>>**) Will Append In The File (Old Content As Well As New Content Will Be There)

Code Example :

```
@echo off
title WritingIntoFiles
echo Enter Your Name
set /p thename=Name :
echo Welcome %thename% >>detail.txt
pause
```

Explanation :

Above Code Will Save Text 'Welcome thename' In **detail.txt** File (Where thename Is The Value Of Variable thename) (**>>** Will Append In The File That Means Old Content As Well As New Content Will Be There In That Text File)

Modifying File Attribute

We Can Also Change Attributes Of File Using Batch Script Programming.

For Adding Read Only Property Command :

attrib +r filename.extension

Example :

attrib +r myfile.txt

For Removing Read Only Property Command :

attrib -r filename.extension

Example :

attrib -r myfile.txt

For Adding Hidden Property Command :

attrib +h filename.extension

Example :

attrib +h myfile.txt

For Removing Hidden Property Command :

attrib -h filename.extension

Example :

attrib -h myfile.txt

Killing Process

To Kill A Process , We Have To Use **taskkill** Command

Command :

taskkill /im processname /f

Where /f Is For Force

Example :

taskkill /im notepad.exe /f

Extracting Values From Registry

To Extract Value From Windows Registry , We Have To Use **reg** Command

Command :

reg query NameOfKey

Example :

reg query HKEY_CURRENT_USER\SOFTWARE\ND

Explanation :

Above Code Will Show All The Values From Specified Key (HKEY_CURRENT_USER\SOFTWARE\ND\ )

Closing Batch Script

To Close Batch Script , We Have To Use **exit** Command

Command :

exit

Code Example :

```
@echo off
title ClosingBatchScript
pause
goto closeit
:closeit
exit
```

ABOUT THE AUTHOR

Narendra Dwivedi Is Currently Pursuing His Engineering Degree In Computer From Pune University. He Is A Web Developer , Ethical Hacker & Software Developer. He Also Releases Courses Related To Technology & Programming On Udemy

Website : www.NarendraDwivedi.Org

www.ingramcontent.com/pod-product-compliance
Ingram Content Group UK Ltd.
Pitfield, Milton Keynes, MK11 3LW, UK
UKHW021938190726
13853UKWH00004B/1512